The P.S. Roadtripper
Electronic Field Trips
for Public Speakers

E. Sam Cox, Ph.D.

Department of Communication
Central Missouri State University
Warrensburg, Missouri 64093
Cox@cmsu1.cmsu.edu

KENDALL/HUNT PUBLISHING COMPANY
4050 Westmark Drive   Dubuque, Iowa 52002

Cover design by Terry McNeeley from an idea by E. Sam Cox.

Copyright © 1998 by E. Sam Cox.

ISBN 0-7872-5420-7

All rights reserved. No part of this publication may be reproduced, stored in a retrieval system, or transmitted, in any form or by any means, electronic, mechanical, photocopying, recording, or otherwise, without the prior written permission of the copyright owner.

Printed in the United States of America
10 9 8 7 6 5 4 3 2 1

Dedication

I dedicate this workbook to the memory of my daughter Christina Dianne. She was a promising and gifted teacher whose example continues to inspire me.

Table of Contents

EFT#1: The Importance of Public Speaking 1

"Before" Activities 1
    Activity 1: The Association Game 2
    Activity 2: Reactions to the Association Experience 2
    Activity 3: Questions 3
    Activity 4: <u>Work America</u> Graph 4
    Activity 5: Tables from 1997 National Study 5
    Second Milers 8

"During" Notes 8

"After" Reflections 10
    Hometown Newspaper Article 12
    EFT Post Assessment 12

EFT#2-- The Role of Listening in Public Communication 13

"Before" Activities 13
    Activity 1: The Association Game 14
    Activity 2: Reactions to the Association Experience 15
    Activity 3: General Student Outcomes Table 15
    Activity 4: Listening Self-Evaluation 18
    Activity 5: Tables from 1997 National Study 19
    Activity 6: Goss Model of Listening 20
    Activity 7: Biased Responses 21
    Second Milers 22

"During" Notes 23

"After" Reflections 24
    Hometown Newspaper Article 26
    EFT Post Assessment

EFT#3 -- Creating a Presentation 29

"Before" Activities 29
    Activity 1: The Association Game 30
    Activity 2: Reactions to the Association Experience 31
    Activity 3: General Student Outcomes Table 31

- Activity 4: General Purpose Statements 32
- Activity 5: Specific Purpose Statements 34
- Activity 5: Thesis Statements 35
- Activity 6: Aristotle's Proofs: Ethos, Pathos, Logos 35
  - Matching 36
  - Evaluate the Usage 36
- Second Milers 38

"During" Notes 38

"After" Reflections 40
- Hometown Newspaper Article 43
- EFT Post Assessment 44

EFT#4 -- Organizing a Presentation 45

"Before" Activities 45
- Activity 1: The Association Game 46
- Activity 2: Reactions to the Association Experience 47
- Activity 3: Trip to Bangor, Maine 47
- Activity 4: Parts of a Presentation 48
- Activity 5: Arrangement Patterns 49
- Activity 6: Coordination, Simplicity, and Subordination 50
- Activity 7: Scrambled Outline 51
- Activity 8: Spidergram 52
- Activity 9: Introductions/Conclusions 53
- Activity 10: Evaluate an Introduction 54
- Activity 11: Produce an Introduction 55
- Activity 12: Produce a Conclusion 56
- Second Milers 56

"During" Notes 57

"After" Reflections 58
- Hometown Newspaper Article 62
- EFT Post Assessment 62

EFT#5—The Importance of Language 63

"Before" Activities 63
- Activity 1: The Association Game 64
- Activity 2: Reactions to the Association Experience 65
- Activity 3: M-A-N 67

Activity 4: Levels of Abstraction	69
Activity 5: Meaning: Denotative versus Connotative	70
Activity 6: Style: Written versus Oral	71
Activity 7: Producing Similes	73
Second Milers	74

"During" Notes ... 74

"After" Reflections ... 76
    Hometown Newspaper Article ... 78
    EFT Post Assessment ... 80

EFT#6—Delivering a Speech ... 81

"Before" Activities ... 81
    Activity 1: The Association Game ... 82
    Activity 2: Reactions to the Association Experience ... 83
    Activity 3: Types of Delivery ... 84
    Activity 4: Do's and Don'ts ... 85
    Activity 5: Vocal Behavior ... 86
    Activity 6: Anxiety 89
    Second Milers ... 89

"During" Notes ... 90

"After" Reflections ... 92
    Hometown Newspaper Article ... 94
    EFT Post Assessment ... 96

EFT#7—Analyzing Your Audience ... 97

"Before" Activities ... 97
    Activity 1: The Association Game ... 98
    Activity 2: Reactions to the Association Experience ... 99
    Activity 3: Audience Adaptation ... 100
    Activity 4: Attitudes and Group Affiliations ... 101
    Activity 5: Features of an Audience Analysis   101
    Activity 6: Persuasive Speech Evaluation Form ... 103
    Second Milers ... 104

"During" Notes 105
"After" Reflections 106
    Tailoring a Topic for Different Audiences 109
    Hometown Newspaper Article 110
    EFT Post Assessment 111

Preface

This workbook is intentionally arranged into Before, During and After activities. These experiences immerse participants in a learning environment that maximizes the exchange of knowledge. The Before activities build a foundation upon which the content of the Electronic Field Trips (EFT's) can be assimilated and assessed. They provide students an orientation to and context for interpreting the video portion of the experience. The During activities are designed to help the participants focus on the relevant and essential elements of the EFT. Finally, the After activities guide participants to reflect upon and apply what has been experienced.

Two years of classroom experience in some 20 sections of Public Speaking emphatically confirms that effective use of EFT's is dependent on them being integrated into the total learning environment. Sticking in a video clip as filler will be just that—filler. But, integration of EFT's into the whole learning environment can excite and motivate students. EFT's help dispel the "ho hum" attitude so often encountered in general education courses like Public Speaking. The most obvious impact of the EFT's has been the change in student attitudes. No longer do I hear students complain that public speaking is just "hoop jumping" or a "useless waste of time since they do not want to be professional speakers." Instead, students are exposed to practitioners from numerous fields and ethnic backgrounds who bridge them to the work world. This experience impresses upon students of the value and utility of the learning regardless of their career path.

During two-weeks at the Teletraining Institute in Stillwater, Oklahoma, I was exposed to the use of electronic field trips (EFT's). While at Stillwater, I co-created an EFT regarding communication apprehension. Stimulated by this experience, the idea of using EFT's in public speaking classes was born. The goal was to transport the class to community professionals who could demonstrate the value and utility of what was being taught in the classroom. With the able assistance of Kristin Brown-Owens, the first version of the EFT's was produced. It consisted of four practitioners, community leaders from rural communities in which four telesites of a public speaking course were located. Aided by John Ong, the second edition was shot and produced. It consists of 25 practitioners who vary greatly in age and occupation.

The initial EFT experience, the JASON Project by the Woods Hole Oceanographic Institute in 1989, stimulated interest in the utilization of EFT's. Then, Garcia, in her 1993 doctoral dissertation,"The Development of the Electronic Field Trip to Strengthen and Enrich Existing K-12 Curriculum," highlighted the key elements for a successful electronic field trip. She stressed the absolute need for Before, During and After activities. She concluded that effective EFT's must provide students with an experience comprised of four components. (1) The first component she labels "print support materials," a phase that precedes the field trip. (2) The orientation phase provides an overview of the total experience and stimulates interest in the upcoming EFT. (3) The third component is the actual electronic field trip itself. (4) The final component she labels the electronic bulletin board where guided reflection occurs. The P.S. Roadtripper utilizes Garcia's model for EFT's.

Finally, the Before, During, and After sections for each EFT capture what R. M. Gagne, L. J. Briggs and W. W. Wagner (1988) in <u>Principles of Instruction</u> call the nine elements in their "Instructional Events Design Model." The Before activities help gain attention, inform the learner of the objective and stimulate recall of prerequisite learning. The During activities present the stimulus and provide learner guidance. The After activities elicit performance, provide feedback, assess the performance and enhance retention and transfer. As H. J. Frieberg and A. Driscoll (1992) in <u>Universal Teaching Strategies</u> note, these elements insure a tight link between teaching and learning.

Acknowledgements

The EFT's and the P.S. Roadtripper workbook would never have occurred without the massive support and encouragement of Kristin Brown-Owens, a bright, insightful and caring teacher who helped me keep the focus on the student. Similarly, the significant improvements between the first and second versions of the EFT's would not have been possible without the brilliant assistance of John Ong. His creative genius repeatedly turned raw ideas into works of art. The support given me by the entire Department of Communication at Central Missouri State University and especially past chair, Dan Curtis, will be forever appreciated. A special thanks is due Terry McNeeley for his wonderful help with the artwork. I am indebted to my wife Dianne for her superb editorial assistance. A special thanks is due my daughter Katie who did my chores so I could devote myself to writing.

Electronic Field Trip #1
The Importance of Public Speaking

You are about to experience an Electronic Field Trip (EFT) with the PS Roadtripper. This field trip is designed to enrich your understanding of the need for public speaking skills. Consider the following reactions by former field trip participants.

"Being able to communicate is extremely important whether it is written or verbal."

"I learned that although I hated to take this class, you have to have good communication skills. By taking this class, I hope to accomplish that."

"All types of people in the business world today need some type of communication skills."

"That not only the speaker but the listener and the message are all three important to relationships."

"Don't treat this class as a joke cause you'll probably need these skills somewhere down the road."

On EFT#1 you will travel to five business locations and visit with five professionals. Like any field trip, there are things that need to be done **before** leaving, **during** the trip and **after** one returns home. To get ready for EFT#1 complete the following activities and read chapters 1 & 3 in Jaffe, C. (1998). Public speaking: Concepts and skills for a diverse society (2nd ed.). Belmont, CA: Wadsworth; which addresses the role of Public Speaking in society as a whole. **Before leaving fill your virtual backpack with the following:**

Activity 1: The Association Game. Read the following phrases and immediately write down connections you see between that word or phrase and public speaking.

Example: <u>Word</u> – Leadership   <u>Association</u> –Courage & confidence

Employable –

Empowering--

Free Society—

Social Responsibility—

Cultural Vehicle—

Activity 2: Reactions to the Association Experience. In dyads or in small groups, share your reactions to the association experience. Taking one concept at a time, reflect on everyone's responses.

    Were there any common responses?

    What did you learn about each other?

    What did you learn about the concepts?

Activity 3: Questions. Write down your answers to the following questions.

What skills do you think will be most important in your career?

List three or four things that you believe will almost always make any employer's top ten list when discussing the knowledge, skills and abilities that make a person employable,

How often, during a typical month, do you think most professionals give presentations?

How do you think business leaders rank the five most highly valued skills that a worker can bring to the workplace?

In addition to career related uses of public speaking, list three other areas where public speaking skills fulfill an important role in society.

A pilot goes through a checklist before each flight, assessing his or her readiness against a checklist. In Activities 1-3 you have prepared. Now in Activities 4 and 5 compare your readiness against a "checklist" of experts.

Activity 4: Work America Graph. Examine this graph provided by the National Alliance of Business *Work America*, Volume 11, Issue 6, July 1994, page 5 and identify the two largest and two smallest gaps between the importance of the skill and finding workers with that skill.

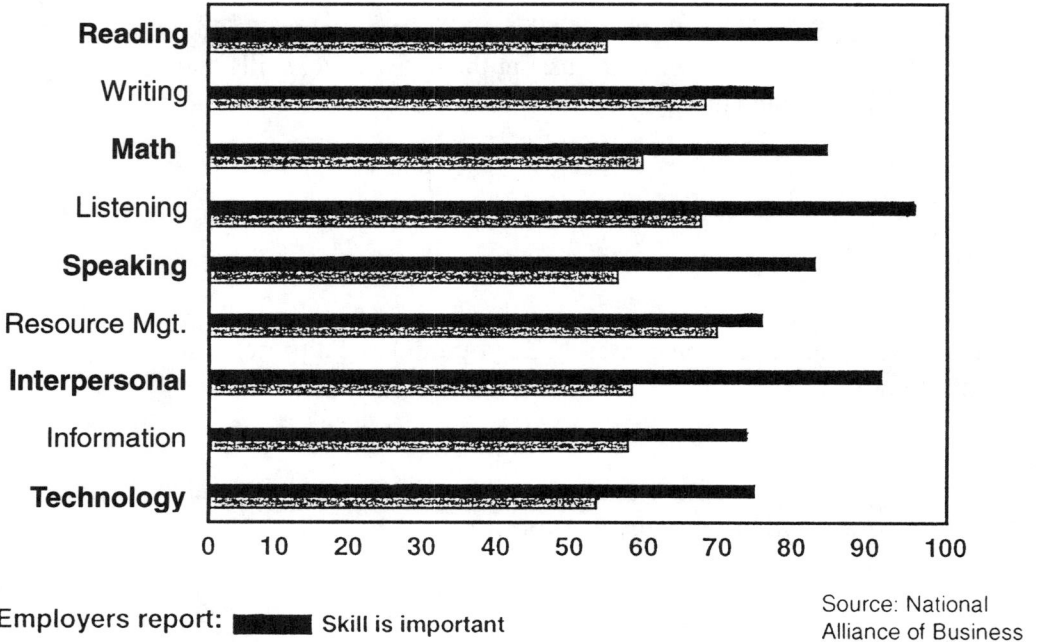

Where are the largest gaps? What might explain the size of these gaps?

Where are the smallest gaps? What might explain the size of these gaps?

Activity 5: Tables from 1997 National Survey. In 1997, Winsor, Curtis, and Stephens replicated their 1989 study by sending questionnaires to 1,000 randomly selected human resource managers in the United States. (For the full report see Winsor, J. L., Curtis, D. B., & Stephens, R. D. (1997). National preferences in business and communication education: A survey update. <u>Journal of the Association for Communication Administration, 3,</u> 170-179.) They produced four tables that summarize what they found related to getting a job, being successful in a job, being equipped for entry-level management, and the profile for an ideal manger.

TABLE 1

Factors Most Important in Helping Graduating College Students Obtain Employment

Rank/Order	Factors/Skills Evaluated	Score	Previous Study Rank
1	Oral (speaking) communication	4.667	1
2	Written communication skills	4.321	4
3	Listening ability	4.293	2
4	Enthusiasm	4.260	3
5	Technical competence	4.176	5
6	Work experience	4.071	8
7	Appearance	3.931	6
8	Poise	3.878	7
9	Resume	3.749	9
10	Part-time or summer employment	3.493	12
11	Specific degree held	3.308	10
12	Leadership in campus/community activities	3.290	14
13	Recommendations	3.248	16
14	Accreditation of program activities	3.194	13
15	Participation in campus/community	3.184	15

From *Journal of the Association for Communication Administration*, No. 3, September 1997 by Winsor, Curtis and Stephens. Copyright © 1997 by Association for Communication Administration. Reprinted by permission.

TABLE 2
Factors/Skills Important For Successful Job Performance

Rank/Order	Factors/Skills Rated as Important	Score	Previous Study Rank
1	Interpersonal/human relations skills	4.593	1
2	Oral (speaking) communication skills	4.515	2
3	Written communication skills	4.346	3
4	Enthusiasm	4.265	5
5	Persistence/determination	4.110	4
6	Technical competence	4.088	6
7	Work experience	3.988	8
8	Personality	3.870	7
9	Poise	3.807	10
10	Dress/grooming	3.750	9
11	Interviewing skills	3.454	11
12	Specific degree held	2.936	12
13	Grade-point average	2.681	14
14	Letters of recommendation	2.604	17
15	Physical attractiveness	2.604	13
16	School attended	2.258	16
	Resume (excluded in current study)		15

TABLE 3
Courses of Importance for Entry-level Managers

Rank/Order	Courses	Score	Previous Study Rank
1	Written communication	4.428	1
2	Interpersonal communication	4.351	2
3	Management	4.043	3
4	Public Speaking	3.936	4
5	Ethics in management	3.930	5
6	Personnel management courses	3.822	6
7	Financial management	3.700	7
8	Marketing	3.480	9
9	Public relations	3.479	12
10	Accounting	3.386	11
11	Mathematics	3.362	10
12	Business law	3.361	17
13	Computer programming	3.346	8
14	Statistics	3.309	14
15	Social and behavioral sciences	3.261	16
16	Production management	3.243	13
17	Economics	3.194	15
18	Humanities, fine and liberal arts	2.859	19
19	Power and technology	2.761	18
20	Mass communication	2.709	20
21	Political science	2.658	21
22	Life sciences	2.536	22

TABLE 4

Ideal Management Profile

Rank/Order	Trait/Skill	Score	Previous Study Rank
1	Ability to listen effectively and counsel	4.662	4
2	Ability to work well with others one-on-one	4.641	1
3	Ability to work well in small groups	4.598	3
4	Ability to gather accurate information from others to make a decision	4.483	2
5	Ability to write effective business reports	4.311	6
6	Ability to give effective feedback (appraisal)	4.293	5
7	Knowledge of job	4.126	7
8	Ability to present a good public image for the organization	4.068	8
9	Ability to use computers	3.928	9
10	Knowledge of finance	3.379	11
11	Knowledge of management theory	3.326	10
12	Knowledge of marketing	3.277	12
13	Knowledge of accounting	3.189	13
14	Ability to use business machines	3.137	14

Study the tables and identify the number of times human communication is mentioned in each table.

Table 1 _____   Table 2 _____   Table 3 _____   Table 4 _____

Write down three conclusions that you draw based on the 1997 study by Winsor, Curtis and Stephens.

Okay, are you ready for the field trip? Your **before** preparations have included five major activities. You brainstormed and shared reactions to some key concepts. You answered questions focused on the role of public speaking in specific settings. You examined the communication skill deficiencies that many workers lack. Finally, you compared your answers to the "checklist" provided by experts and business leaders.

But wait! Is there anything else you would want to do before you leave on the field trip? If so, jot it down and share it with your instructor and/or a classmate. It is always unsettling to leave home with the nagging feeling that you left something you wanted to take.

Second Milers: If you want more than the minimum preparation for EFT#1, examine the comments about the roles and functions of public speaking in chapter 1 in Osborn, M., & Osborn, S. (1994). Public speaking (3rd ed.). Boston: Houghton Mifflin; or read chapters 1 and 2 in Lucas, S. L. (1995). The art of public speaking (5th ed.). New York: McGraw-Hill.

DURING

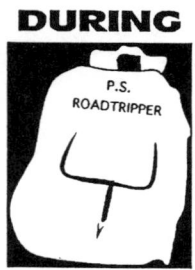

In EFT #1 we will visit with a banker, a receptionist, a sales representative, a graphic designer/animator and with an education coordinator for a salon supply company. The question that we will ask each practitioner is **"What skills are most important in your position?"**

Feel free to also take notes during each visit. Brief notes will enable you to better discuss the following questions with your classmates.

Guess how often each of these people gives presentations in a given month?

Banker___ Receptionist____ Sales Rep.____ Designer____ Coordinator_____

Note which of the following each person addressed. Place a large X under the category for EACH person who mentions the role of public speaking in that area.

	General Importance	Being Valued	Employable	Empowered
Banker				
Receptionist				
Sales Representative				
Graphic Designer				
Coordinator				

Key points made by each person interviewed.

Banker:

Receptionist:

Sales representative:

Graphic designer/animator:

Education coordinator:

Preparation must be made **before** taking the trip and important questions must be asked **during** the field trip. But nothing is more important than what happens **after** the field trip. Critical reflection upon the knowledge gained is what makes all the effort worthwhile.

Reflections. What did you personally learn from this Electronic Field Trip?

How often do these practitioners actually give presentations?

Banker____ Receptionist____ Sales Rep____ Designer____ Coordinator____

What does that suggest regarding the utility of public speaking skills for success in diverse careers? your career?

To what extent do these practitioners confirm or illustrate what you read in Work America and The Journal of the Association for Communication Administration? Explain your answers.

Identify which person in the field trip you believe most insightfully addressed each of the following. Be prepared to provide reasons for your choice.

    Public speaking skills and being employable—

    The role of public speaking and personal empowerment—

    Social responsibility in a free society—

    Presentation skills being highly valued –

Based upon the Electronic Field Trip and your text's discussion of the role of public communication in society, has your attitude toward this course changed? If so, how? If not, why not?

Hometown Newspaper Article. You have been invited by your hometown newspaper to write an advice column for those planning to go to college. Combine your experience on the EFT with all your knowledge about the roles and functions of public speaking in a person's life. Write a brief article that addresses at least three of the following concepts as they relate to public speaking: employable, free society, social responsibility, highly valued, cultural vehicle and empowering. Feel free to use the practitioners from the EFT as "eye witness" accounts. Your objective is to provide three distinct and compelling reasons why college students should take Public Speaking. (Your instructor may want to collect these and share a few with the entire class.)

EFT Post Assessment. Finally, what, if anything, would you change about this EFT to make it a better educational experience? No one can make a better post-assessment of the content and process of this field trip than you, since you took the field trip.

You can now unpack your backpack and anticipate your next Electronic Field Trip.

Electronic Field Trip #2
Listening

You are about to experience an Electronic Field Trip (EFT) with the PS Roadtripper. This field trip is designed to increase your understanding of the need for and functions of listening—the forgotten half of communication. Listen to what former field trip participants have said about EFT#2.

"I learned how important listening is. Every job requires good listening skills. Never thought about it, but you could lose a job or a position if you do not have good listening skills."

"Listening is very important. If listening does not occur most jobs would be lost."

"Being a good listener is essential. Listening is vital. So discipline yourself to hear."

"I don't know if anything needs to be improved. I found the EFT very interesting."

On EFT#2 you will travel to six unique and vastly different business locations. Like any trip, there are things that must be done **before** leaving, **during** the trip and **after** one returns home. To get ready for EFT#2 complete the following activities and read chapter 4 in Jaffe, C. (1998). Public speaking: Concepts and skills for a diverse society (2nd ed.). Belmont, CA: Wadsworth which addresses the vital role. **Before leaving fill your virtual backpack with the following:**

Activity 1: The Association Game. Read the following phrases and immediately, without reflection or deliberation, write down your initial reactions.

Example: Phrase---Difficult to understand   Associations---unclear and uses technical language

Listening and critical thinking--

Attending to messages---

Comprehending what is heard---

Analyzing what is heard---

Evaluating what is spoken---

Responding to messages---

Active listening---

Importance of listening---

Listening barriers--

Ways to remember—

Activity 2: Reactions to the Association Experience. In dyads or in small groups, share your reactions to the association experience. Taking one concept at a time, reflect on everyone's responses.

    What, if any, were the common responses?

    What did you learn about each other?

    What did you learn about the concepts?

Activity 3: General Student Outcomes Table. The Faculty Senate University Studies Committee identified four generalized student outcomes for all University Studies courses: Communicating, Thinking, Valuing and Interacting. Public Speaking (SpCm 1000) is in Division I: Intellectual Skills (see page 36 in the 1998-2000 Catalog) and is designed to help students achieve the outcomes of Communicating and Thinking.

Examine the following table that lists the knowledge and/or understanding outcomes a student is expected to achieve as well as application outcomes for Communicating and Thinking.

GENERAL STUDENT OUTCOMES
(Some outcomes are abbreviated)
Central Missouri State University, December, 1990

	Communicating --Reading --Listening --Speaking --Writing --Quantitative literacy --Visual --Computer	Thinking --Analysis --Logic --Critical --Creative --Problem Solving --Value-based
Knowledge /Understanding	A Student: --recognizes the four basic principles of communication --uses standard English --avoids errors that make a negative impression on an audience --recognizes the need to adjust communication to an audience --recognizes that clear communication requires clear thinking --recognizes the purpose, main idea & thesis of a communication --learns the rules for computing & communicating quantitative data --identifies the meaning of quantitative data	A Student: --learns the vocabulary & concepts in meta-thinking --makes precise & detailed observations --recognizes & defines a problem using a process --uses meta-thinking in making arguments --summarizes another's & one's own argument --recognizes that the disciplinary, cultural, historical, and philosophical contexts of an argument may vary --identifies & develops alternative problem-solving strategies --values critical thinking & creative thinking in oneself and others --reserves judgment when insufficient evidence for a conclusion exists
Application	A student: --applies the criteria for effective communication to assess the communication of self & others --employs computers in communicating language & quantitative data --employs a variety of audio/visual media in communication --adapts communication to a variety of audiences --applies the four basic principles of communication in variety of contexts --employs an explicit thesis to structure a communication --employs various organizational structures in a variety of communications --employs quantitative data in communicating	A student: --evaluates the strength of other's & own thinking in various contexts & disciplinary frameworks --assesses the validity & adequacy of evidence --assesses own problem-solving processes --employs both induction & deduction --analyzes & employs both quantitative & qualitative evidence in arguments --generates & evaluates alternative strategies for solving problems in several disciplines

Mark each knowledge/understanding outcome for Communicating that seems related to listening? How many did you mark?

Mark each knowledge/understanding outcome for Thinking that seems related to listening? How many did you mark?

Mark each application outcome for Communicating that seems related to listening? How many did you mark?

Mark each application outcome for Thinking that seems related to listening? How many did you mark?

Using your Public Speaking course syllabus, identify every course outcome related to listening. Write them below.

Using all the preceding data answer the question, "Why do you think Public Speaking (SpCm 1000) is listed under Intellectual Skills?"

Activity 4: Listening Self-Evaluation.*

How often do you indulge in the following ten bad listening habits? Rate yourself very honestly and carefully on each item below.

HABIT	FREQUENCY					SCORE
	Almost Always	Usually	Sometimes	Seldom	Almost Never	
1. Giving in to mental distractions						
2. Giving in to physical distractions						
3. Trying to remember everything a speaker says						
4. Rejecting a topic as uninteresting before hearing the speaker						
5. Faking paying attention						
6. Jumping to conclusions about what a speaker means						
7. Deciding a speaker is wrong before hearing everything he or she has to say						
8. Judging a speaker on the basis of his or her personal appearance						
9. Not paying attention to a speaker's evidence						
10. Focusing on delivery rather than on what the speaker says						

How to score:

For every "almost always" checked, give yourself a score of	2
For every "usually" checked, give yourself a score of	4
For every "sometimes" checked, give yourself a score of	6
For every "seldom" checked, give yourself a score of	8
For every "almost never" checked, give yourself a score of	10

TOTAL SCORE INTERPRETATION:
        Below 70 – You need to improve your listening.
        From 71-90 – You listen about average.
        From 91 and above – You listen unusually well.

*Adapted from "Analysis of Your Bad Listening Habits" in Steil, L. K., Barker, L. L., & Watson, K. W. (1983). Effective listening: Key to your success. Reading, MA: Addison-Wesley, pp. 57-58.

In groups of 3 or 4 compare your scores on the Listening Self-Evaluation.

What, if any, are the common areas of weakness?

What, if any, are the common areas of strength?

Write down three reasons why you believe your group had common areas of weakness or common areas of strength or did not have any common areas.

Activity 5: Tables from 1997 National Study. Examine the tables by Winsor, Curtis and Stephens in EFT#1. Answer the following questions.

How important is listening according to the two national surveys?

Identify the places where effective listening seems to be taken for granted.

Activity 6: Goss Model of Listening. Examine the Goss model of listening. Compare your answers to the preceding three questions about your strengths and/or weaknesses with the following information.

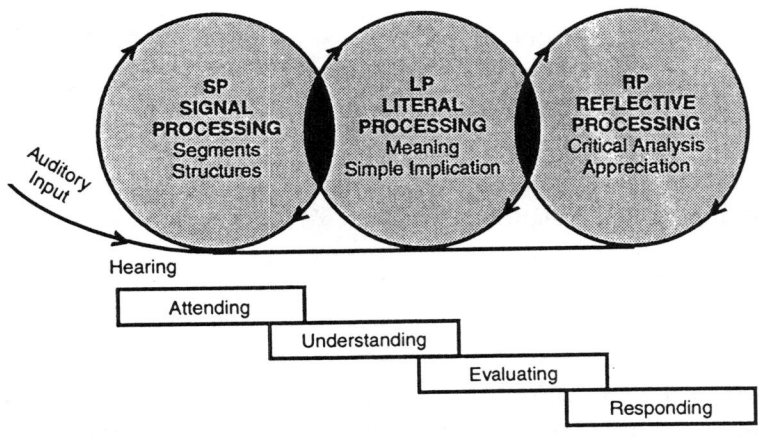

Adapted from Goss, 1982, taken from *Improving Listening Abilities* by James J. Floyd.

Identify where most of your individual listening strengths lie? In Signal Processing? In Literal Processing? In Reflective Processing? Explain why.

Identify where most of your individual listening weaknesses lie? In Signal Processing? In Literal Processing? In Reflective Processing? Explain why.

Using the model by Goss and with help from your classmates, generate three specific actions you can take to help improve your "Attending?"

　　　1.

　　　2.

　　　3.

Compare your three specific actions to improve your "Attending" with this list.

Improving Your Ability to Pay Attention*

- Resist the temptation to daydream

- Reduce environmental distraction

- Ignore internal (self-generated) distractions

- Refuse to be distracted by speaker appearance and mannerisms

- Repeatedly remind yourself to focus on the message

---

*From Floyd, J. J. (1998). Improving listening abilities. Dubuque, IA: Kendall/Hunt, p. 46.

Which actions suggested by Floyd are similar to your suggestions?

Which are different?

Activity 7: Biased Responses. Read the following illustration. After you read the scenario, match the types of biased responses that are likely to occur with the descriptions of those responses.*

> Let us assume that one of us is listening to a friend who is talking about abortion. Let us assume, further, that the listener's religious training has taught him or her that abortion is a sin, that it is exactly the same thing as murder, and that it is never justified. The person speaking is also opposed to abortion but not as strongly as the listener. At one point early in the discussion the speaker says that we have to have some understanding for people who sincerely believe that abortion is a matter of personal choice. At this point the listener may reject the speaker, deciding that he or she is in favor of abortion on demand and is, consequently, an immoral person. This response may negatively affect the listener throughout the remainder of the conversation. Our listener may begin to distort the rest of the speaker's remarks in a variety of ways.

1. _____ "Filtering"

a. By deciding that any anti-abortion statements were not sincere or were stated simply to throw the listener off guard.

2. _____ "Assimilation-contrast"

b. By simply not processing some of the content.

3. _____ "Deletion-addition"

c. By insisting that the speaker made statements or took stands which he or she did not take.

4. _____ "Rationalization"

d. By deleting message elements, or by adding or inserting elements into the message that were not there.

*The senario and descriptions are from Floyd, J. J. (1998). Improving listening abilities. Dubuque, IA: Kendall/Hunt, p. 23; the terms are from Makay, J. J. & Brown, W. R. (1972) in The rhetorical dialogue: Contemporary concepts and cases. Dubuque, IA: Brown.

Okay, are you ready for the field trip? Your **before** preparations have included five major activities. You brainstormed and shared reactions to some key concepts and then examined the outcomes for Public Speaking as a University Studies course. You answered questions focused on the role of listening in business settings, took a self-test and then reflected on your strengths and weaknesses. Finally, you read a scenario that led to an examination of barriers to good listening.

But wait! Is there anything else you would want to do before you leave on the field trip? If so, jot it down and share it with your instructor and/or a classmate. It is always unsettling to leave home with the nagging feeling that you left something home you wanted to take.

Second Milers: For those who like to go the second mile, excellent additional information can be found in the following public speaking textbooks. Examine chapter 8 in Kearney, P., & Plax, T. G. (1996). Public speaking in a diverse society. Mountain View, CA: Mayfield; or study chapter 3 in Zarefsky, D. (1996). Public speaking: Strategies for success. Boston: Allyn & Bacon.

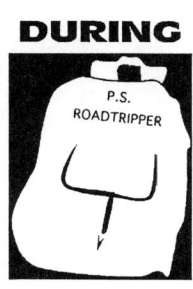

DURING

Now that you have made the necessary preparations, let's take the field trip. In this EFT we will visit with an investor services representative, the owner of a cleaning company, a TV production assistant, a videographer, a news receptionist, and a retail credit manager. We will ask them: **"How important is listening to your position and what does it mean to be a good listener?"**

Feel free to take notes during each visit. Brief notes will enable you to better discuss the following questions with your classmates.

Note which of the following each person addressed. Place a large X under the category for EACH person who mentions that aspect of listening.

	Attending	Understand	Evaluate	Respond	Barriers
Investor					
Owner					
Prod. Assist.					
Videographer					
Manager					

Key points made by each person interviewed.

Investor:

Owner:

Production Assistant:

Videographer:

Receptionist:

Manager:

Preparation must be made **before** taking the trip and important questions must be asked **during** the field trip. But nothing is more important than what happens **after** the field trip. Critical reflection upon the knowledge gained is what makes all the effort worthwhile.

Reflections. What did you learn from this Electronic Field Trip?

To what extent do these practitioners confirm or illustrate what you read before you took the field trip? For example, compare what they said with the Goss model or with Floyd's recommended actions or with the biases that hinder effective listening. Explain.

Identify which person in the field trip you believe most insightfully addressed each of the following and explain why.

Listening and critical thinking–

Attending to messages—

Comprehending what is heard—

Analyzing what is heard—

Evaluating what is spoken—

Responding to messages—

Active listening—

Importance of listening—

Listening barriers--

Ways to remember—

Based upon the Electronic Field Trip and your text's discussion of the roles and functions of listening in society, has your attitude toward public speaking changed? If so, how? If not, why not?

Hometown Newspaper Article. You have been invited by your hometown newspaper to write an advice column for those planning to go to college. Combining your experience on the EFT with all your knowledge about the roles and functions of listening in a person's life, write a brief article that addresses at least three of the following concepts: active listening, listening barriers, attending, understanding, a vital skill, analyzing, evaluating, responding, critical thinking or remembering. Your objective is to show how being an accomplished listener will enable you to become a better public speaker. (Your instructor may want to collect these and share a few with the entire class.)

EFT Post Assessment. Finally, what, if anything, would you change about this EFT to make it a better educational experience? No one can make a better post-assessment of the content and process of this field trip than you, since you took the field trip.

You can now unpack the rest of your bags and await your next Electronic Field Trip.

Electronic Field Trip #3
Creating a Presentation

You are about to experience an Electronic Field Trip (EFT) with the PS Roadtripper. This field trip is designed to increase your understanding of and ability to generate an effective presentation. Listen to what former field trip participants have said about EFT#3.

> "I learned that it is important to research your topic in order to gather information to support it. You can acquire this from books, experts in the field, and through talking to people that have had personal experience with the topic."

> "I learned how and where to find support materials as well as how to utilize resources with topics."

> "I learned that most of the interviewees felt that consulting those with experience and knowledge and knowing what point they wanted to get across were two important skills in gathering information."

> "I learned that you need to research your topic and use a lot of different resources to get information."

On EFT#3 you will travel to five unique and vastly different business locations. Like any trip, there are things that must be done **before** leaving, **during** the trip and **after** one returns home. To get ready for EFT#3 you need to complete the following activities and read chapters 2, 6, 7 & 8 in Jaffe, C. (1998). <u>Public speaking: Concepts and skills for a diverse society</u> (2nd ed.). Belmont, CA: Wadsworth which address topics like selecting and researching a topic, steps in speech preparation, and using supporting in a speech. **Before leaving fill your virtual backpack with the following:**

Activity 1: The Association Game. Read the following words or phrases and immediately, without reflection or deliberation, write connections you see between each concept and creating a presentation.

Example: <u>Word</u>--Brainstorming   <u>Association</u>--throwing out a bunch of ideas

Research–

Topic selection—

Analyzing information—

Support for claims—

Invention—

Facts—

Testimony—

Purpose statement—

Primary sources---

Secondary sources—

Record accurately--

Activity 2: Reactions to the Association Experience. In dyads or in small groups, share your reactions to the association experience. Taking one concept at a time, reflect on everyone's responses.

Were there any common responses?

What did you learn about each other?

What did you learn about the concepts?

How would you begin to create a successful speech?

Activity 3: General Student Outcomes Table. Go to EFT#2 and find the table of the Generalized Student Outcomes for Communicating and Thinking for all University Studies courses (p. 16).

Carefully re-examine that table. This time mark each knowledge/understanding outcome for Thinking that seems related to creating a presentation? How many did you mark?

Mark each knowledge/understanding outcome for Communicating that seems related to creating a presentation? How many did you mark?

Mark each application outcome for Thinking that seems related to creating a presentation? How many did you mark?

Mark each application outcome for Communicating that seems related to creating a presentation? How many did you mark?

Using the syllabus for your Public Speaking course, identify every departmentally approved course outcome that seems related to creating a presentation. Write them below.

Meet with two or three classmates and identify the Generalized Outcomes for Communicating and Thinking that Public Speaking is designed to address? Write all the outcomes upon which there was unanimous agreement.

Activity 4: General Purpose Statements. A vital beginning step in the construction of a speech is to determine the purpose for giving the speech. Three General Purpose Statements are: To Inform; To Persuade; and, To Entertain.

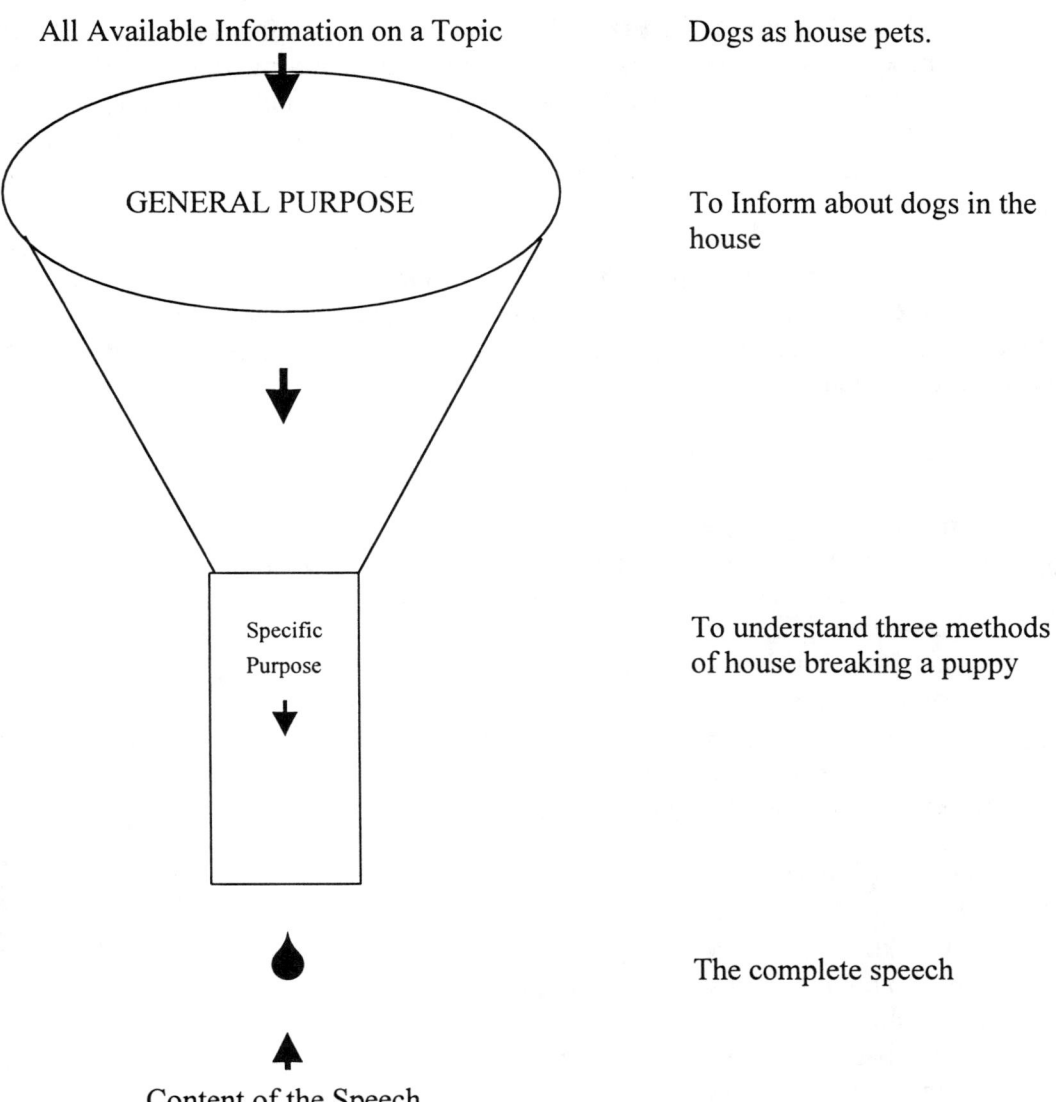

Write 3 General Purpose Statements on the topic of food.

    1.   To Inform

    2.   To Persuade

Activity 5: Specific Purpose Statements. A clearly worded specific purpose statement is the key to selecting information as you prepare a presentation. Consider this example of a Specific Purpose Statement. "I would like my audience to know the three steps to house breaking a puppy." The following exercise provides pre-field trip practice with specific purpose statements.

Match the following Specific Purpose Statements with the most appropriate General Purpose Statement. Note how the Specific Purpose Statements are complete sentences, contain one idea, are written in the infinitive form, and state a desired response in the audience.

_____ I would like my audience to join Amnesty International.

_____ I would like my audience to understand the characteristics of the five common types of zone defenses in basketball.

_____ I would like my audience to laugh at my experience as a waiter.

_____ I would like my audience to understand that oral and written communication skills are the keys to career advancement in all fields.

_____ I would like my audience to believe that drug testing by business and industry should be prohibited.

_____ I would like my audience to laugh at reasons people do not major in speech communication.

_____ I would like my audience to understand the three basic forms of mystery stories.

_____ I would like my audience to sign up for Foundations of Communication Theory.

_____ I would like my audience to be amused by my portrayal of an over-the-hill football player.

A. To Inform

B. To Persuade

C. To Entertain

Activity 6: Thesis Statements. The next step is to consider differences between **specific** purpose statements and **thesis** statements? Compare the following examples.

Specific
Purpose: I would like the audience to understand three major methods for house breaking a puppy.

Versus

Thesis: Puppies can be house broken by using the paper, the cage or the "48-20" training method.

AND

Specific
Purpose: I would like the audience to major or minor in speech communication.

Versus

Thesis: Speech Communication majors and minors receive an excellent liberal arts education, have the most sought after entry-level skills, and have the background needed for advancement in all jobs.

What are major differences between specific purpose statements and thesis statements?

Activity 7: Aristotle's Proofs--Ethos, Logos, Pathos. Now that you have collected your thoughts about purpose statements and thesis statements, you are ready to rummage through Aristotle's proofs. Ethos, logos, and pathos are tools you will want to pack.

Matching: Match the following.* (A, B & C will be used several times.)

_____ appeals to what an audience wants   A. Ethos

_____ the trustworthiness of the speaker   B. Logos

_____ appeals through reasoning   C. Pathos

_____ appeals to evidence

_____ the knowledge of the speaker

_____ the emotions of the audience

_____ the character of the speaker

_____ reliance on data

_____ the charisma of the speaker

*To check your answers see Jaffe, C. (1998). Public speaking: Concepts and skills for a diverse society (2nd ed.). Belmont, CA: Wadsworth, pages 291-308.

Evaluate the Usage: Read the following, the introduction and the story, to evaluate the uses of ethos, logos and pathos.

Dr. James Dobson, who earned his Ph.D. from the University of Southern California, was a practicing psychologist for many years. Then, Dr. Dobson launched his Focus on the Family Ministry. It has been 21 years since he aired his first broadcast of "Focus on the Family," on 24 radio stations around the country. Today, Dr. Dobson's ministry is truly a multimedia outreach that is known throughout the United States and around the world. In a 1997 article in his Focus on the Family Bulletin, 10 (2), (no page number), Dr. Dobson wrote an article titled "Mutual Admission."

Mutual Admiration

     Our sense of self-respect is often based on the reactions, positive or negative, of those around us. That is especially true in the intimate context of marriage.
     Consider Peter Foster, a Royal Air Force pilot in World War II. He flew a Hurricane, a fighter with a design flaw—the engine, mounted in the front, had fuel lines

---

From *Focus on the Family* by Dr. James Dobson. Copyright © 1997 by Focus on the Family. Reprinted by permission.

running past the cockpit. If hit, the pilot would be engulfed in flames before he could eject. The consequences were tragic.

Some pilots caught in that inferno would undergo up to 20 surgeries to reconstruct their faces. Peter Foster was one of those downed pilots whose face was burned beyond recognition. But Foster had the support of his family and the love of his fiancée. She told him that nothing had changed except a few millimeters of skin. Two years later they were married.

Foster said of his wife, "She became my mirror. She gave me anew image of myself. When I look at her, she give me a loving smile that tells me I'm OK."

That's how a marriage should work. It can be a mutual admiration society that builds the self-esteem of both partners and overlooks a million flaws that could otherwise be destructive. There's a word for that kind of commitment: We call it love.

Identify uses of ethos, logos and pathos in the story and in the introduction of Dr. Dobson.

--Ethos

--Pathos

--Logos

Which of Aristotle's proofs is most common in this example?

Write any questions you have about using ethos, logos and pathos.

Are you ready for the field trip? Your **before** preparations have included seven major activities. You checked your knowledge of key concepts by playing the association game. You examined the outcomes for Public Speaking as a University Studies course. You reflected on your old process for creating a presentation and then worked with purpose statements and thesis statements. Finally, you reviewed Aristotle's three artistic proofs and wrote questions for the practitioners to be visited on EFT#3.

But wait! Is there anything else you would want to do before you leave on the field trip? If so, jot it down and share it with your instructor and/or a classmate. It is always unsettling to leave home with the nagging feeling that you left something home you wanted to take.

Second Milers: For those who like to go the second mile, excellent additional information about how to create a compelling presentation can be found in the following public speaking textbooks. See chapters 2, 4 & 5 in Verderber, R. F. (1994). The challenge of effective speaking (9th ed.). Belmont, CA: Wadsworth; or study chapters 4 & 5 in Ayres, J. & Miller, J. (1994). Effective public speaking. Madison, WI: Brown & Benchmark.

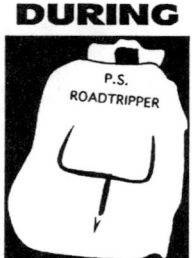

DURING

Now that you have made the necessary preparations, let's take the field trip. In this EFT we will visit with a human resources specialist, the owner of a cleaning company, a TV production assistant, a videographer, and a development coordinator. We will ask: **"How do you go about collecting information to produce a compelling presentation?"**

Feel free to take notes during each visit. Brief notes will enable you to better discuss the following questions with your classmates.

Note which of the following each person addressed. Place a large X under the category for EACH person who mentions that aspect of creating a presentation.

	Research	Purpose	Topic Selection	Resources
HR Specialist				
Owner				
Production Assistant				
Videographer				
Coordinator				

Key points made by each person interviewed.

HR Specialist:

Owner:

Production Assistant:

Videographer:

Coordinator:

Preparation must be made **before** taking the trip and important questions must be asked **during** the field trip. But nothing is more important than what happens **after** the field trip. Critical reflection upon the knowledge gained is what makes all the effort worthwhile.

Reflections. What did you learn from this Electronic Field Trip?

To what extent do these practitioners confirm or illustrate what you read before you took the field trip?

Identify which person in the field trip you believe most insightfully addressed each of the following. Provide reasons for your choices.

Research--

Topic selection—

Analyzing information—

Support for claims—

Invention—

Facts—

Testimony—

Purpose statement—

Primary sources---

Secondary sources—

Record accurately--

In groups of 3-5, complete the following. You are to speak to the University President and his cabinet on the topic of security measures on campus.

Generate a General Purpose Statement:

Generate a Specific Purpose Statement:

What kind of supporting materials do you need? Explain why.

Where would you go to get these materials? Explain why.

Produce a Thesis Statement for your presentation.

Based upon your experiences before, during and after Electronic Field Trip #3, do you feel more confident you can produce an effective speech? If so, why? If not, why not?

Hometown Newspaper Article. You have been invited by your hometown newspaper to write an advice column for those planning to go to college. Combining your experience on the EFT with all your knowledge about how to create a presentation, write a brief article that addresses at least three of the following concepts: research, topic selection, analyzing information, support for claims, invention, facts, testimony, purpose statement, primary sources, secondary sources, or accurate recording. Feel free to use the practitioners from the EFT as "eye witness" resources. Your objective is to give aspiring college students advice on creating an effective presentation when applying for major scholarships. (Your instructor may want to collect these and share a few with the entire class.)

EFT Post Assessment. Finally, what, if anything, would you change about this EFT to make it a better educational experience? Remember that no one can make a better post-assessment of the content and process of this field trip than you, since you took the field trip.

You can now unpack your bags and await your next Electronic Field Trip.

Electronic Field Trip #4
Organizing a Presentation

You are about to experience an Electronic Field Trip (EFT) with the PS Roadtripper. This field trip is designed to improve your ability to organize selected information into an effective presentation. Listen to what former field trip participants have said about EFT#4.

> *"I learned that a good presentation should have good visual aids, good organization, clear points and ideas, and proper evaluation of the audience."*

> *"I learned that an outline should be detailed and contain key points. That you need to keep the end product in mind and then decide steps to accomplish those goals."*

> *"Starting out with an outline of your speech is the most important part of organizing the speech. The detailed outline is very important. Then deciding what kind of language to use and determining who will be the audience."*

> *"I learned that you must know what it is you want them to know and how to get them to learn it."*

On EFT#4 you will travel to five unique and vastly different locations. Like any trip, there are things that must be done **before** leaving, **during** the trip and **after** one returns home. To get ready for EFT#4 complete the following activities and read chapters 9, 10 & 11 in Jaffe, C. (1998). Public speaking: Concepts and skills for a diverse society (2nd ed.). Belmont, CA: Wadsworth. **Before leaving fill your virtual backpack with the following:**

Activity 1: The Association Game. Without reflection or deliberation, write the connections you see between each concept and organizing a presentation.

Example: Word--Subordination   Association--the placement of minor points under a major point

Balance–

Arrangement—

Conclusion—

Central idea—

Organizational patterns—

Coordination—

Introduction—

Outlining---

Orderly—

Body--

Transitions---

Activity 2: Reactions to the Association Experience. In dyads or in small groups, share your reactions to the association experience. Taking one concept at a time, reflect on everyone's responses.

Were there any common responses?

What did you learn about each other?

What did you learn about the concepts?

Activity 3: Trip to Bangor, Maine. You have been given one month to get from San Diego, California to Bangor, Maine. All expenses will be paid and no questions will be asked. You may take up to four people with you and may travel any route and by any mode you desire. The only stipulations are that you MUST arrive in Bangor, Maine exactly one month later and you must answer the following five questions prior to leaving.

Question #1 – What will you take with you?

Question #2 – What routes will you take?

Question #3 – How will you travel?

Question #4 – With whom will you travel?

Question #5 – Why will you go this way?

What do you think this experience has to do with organizing a presentation?

Examine the course syllabus and identify the outcome most related to your "dream" trip to Bangor, Maine. Explain why.

Activity 4: Parts of a Presentation. The next step in the "before" process will be more focused and you should be as deliberate and reflective as possible. Write your answers to the following questions.

Name the three main parts to any presentation.

How does this old adage relate to the parts of a presentation? "Tell'em what you're going to tell'em. Tell'em. Tell'em what you told 'em."

The best way to organize a speech, once you have brainstormed for potential ideas, is to start with the body of the speech. Arrangement of the information within the body is like planning your trip dream trip from San Diego to Bangor--it requires a carefully selected plan to get you to a predetermined destiny.

What do we call the predetermined destination in a presentation? (See EFT#3, pages 32-34 for help if needed.)

Activity 5: Arrangement Patterns. Take the following quiz about arrangement patterns to help assess your current knowledge. Select the BEST answer.

1. The topical arrangement will…
   a. use a time line to sequence the information.
   b. arrange the information by place or location.
   c. be used when the points to do not need to be presented in any order.
   d. a & b
   e. b & c

2. The disposition of a speech in a problem-solution format will…
   a. focus on the arguments in favor of and the arguments against the proposal.
   b. proceed in a chronological manner.
   c. explore some of the reasons or causes for the dilemma.
   d. look like a "wave" if diagrammed.
   e. provide calls for action that will resolve a dilemma.

3. Narrative patterns are different than traditional patterns in that they…
   a. are not clear.
   b. are hard t follow.
   c. are easier to produce.
   d. are confusing.
   e. none of the above.

4. If a person addresses the reasons for a crisis they most likely using…
   a. a spatial organizational pattern.
   b. a chronological outline.
   c. a topical order.
   d. a causal disposition.
   e. the exemplum arrangement.

* To check your answers see Jaffe, C. (1998). <u>Public speaking: Concepts and skills for a diverse society</u> (2nd ed.). Belmont, CA: Wadsworth, pages 150-164.

Activity 6: Coordination, Simplicity, and Subordination. The next thing to check before leaving on the field trip is your understanding of the principles upon which ANY arrangement pattern is built. Match the following items.

_____ arrangement of data from most important to least important   A. Coordination

_____ each heading contains only one idea   B. Simplicity/Singularity

_____ movement from very specific to very general   C. Subordination

_____ relation between main points and subpoints

_____ points that are about equal in importance reflect

_____ supporting material is _____ to a main point

_____ the relation between parts of the whole and the whole

_____ the relation between a series of causes to each other

_____ a list of functions in relation to one of several jobs

_____ the relation between a series of illustrations of one of three causes

_____ the use of Roman numerals, capital letters and Arabic numbers reflect

    *To check your answers see Osborn, M. & Osborn, S. (1994). <u>Public speaking</u> (3rd ed.). Boston: Houghton Mifflin, pages 215-217.

Activity 7: Scrambled Outline. In the left-hand column below is a partially blank outline for the body of a speech. The topic is the shortage of nurses in the United States. In the right-hand column, arranged in random order, are the subpoints and subsubpoints to fill in the outline. Choose the appropriate subpoint or subsubpoint for each blank in the outline.

Outline	Subpoints and Subsubpoints

I. Our nation's hospitals are suffering a severe shortage of nurses.
  A.
 	
  B.
 	
  C.
 	
II. There are several causes for this serious shortage of nurses.
  A.
 	
    1.
 	
    2.
 	
  B.
 	
  C.
	• A second cause of the shortage is that nurses are reluctant to stay on the job because of poor working hours that include nights and weekends.
	• According to statistics released by the American Hospital Association, the nurse shortage nationwide has reached an alarming 100,000.
	• A Cincinnati General Hospital nurse says, "You've got so many forms to fill out that you have a hard time getting out of the nursing station to see your patients."
	• Nationally, the average salary for a nurse is $5.78 an hour, or about the same as many supermarket checkout clerks get.
	• The major cause of the shortage is that nurses pay is low in relation t their responsibilities.
	• As another nurse put it, "I'm a nurse because I like to work with people. I don't want to be turned into a paper pusher."
	• Another statistic, this one from the National Association of Nurse Recruiters, warns that the average hospital has 37 full-time nursing positions vacant.
	• A third cause of the shortage is that nurses are burdened with excessive paperwork.
	• According to the American Journal of Nursing, there is a mere $2,000 average difference between the salary of a beginning nurse and one with 20 years of experience.
	• Hospitals in Denver, New York and Miami have had to reduce services because of a lack of nurses.

Compare your outline with at least one other person's outline to check how well each of you applied the principles of subordination and coordination. Can the scrambled outline about nursing be arranged differently without violating the principles? Explain.

Activity 8: Spidergram. Now you are ready to dive into a "Spidergram." Kevin James Brown, the author of "Spidergrams," in the Spring 1990 issue of <u>Speech Communication Teacher</u> explains that "Spidergrams consist of drawing a series of boxes big enough to contain one word" (p. 4). He goes on to explain that a "Spidergram" is "a graphic illustration of a technique for outlining" (p. 5). Are you ready to try it?

Take out a blank sheet of paper. In the very middle of your paper draw a box about like this one.

Then, write the word "Dog" in your box.

Now draw four boxes around the central box like this.

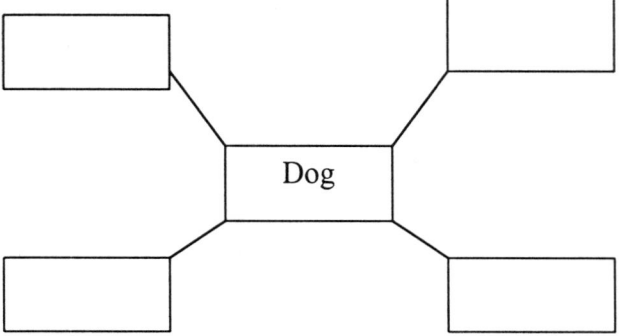

The next step is to fill in each of the four surrounding boxes with a type of dog. Go ahead; fill in your boxes. Put hunting dogs in one box.

Okay, add boxes around each type of dog and fill those boxes in with specific types. Around hunting dogs you could put bird dogs, deer dogs, squirrel dogs and rabbit dogs.

Do you understand how this works? You could continue by placing specific breeds of bird dogs around the bird dog box. And, you could then take one breed, say English Pointers, and place boxes around that box in which you could write things like specific blood lines or colors.

It is time to pack the lesson for our field trip.

    What do the boxes represent?

    What do the lines between the boxes portray?

    What is the relationship between all the boxes directly linked to one box?

    What is the relationship between three boxes along three connecting lines?

    How does the principle of simplicity fit with your "Spidergram?"

Activity 9: Introductions/Conclusions. To help you decide what else you need to take on EFT#4, match the following items. The same answer will be used several times and the question may have multiple answers.*

_____ signal the end	A. Function of a Conclusion
_____ set a tone for the speech	B. Function of an Introduction
_____ a quotation	C. Type of Introduction
_____ an appeal for action	D. Type of Conclusion
_____ capture attention	
_____ summarize	
_____ personal reference/story	

_____ tie to the introduction
_____ secure goodwill and respect
_____ suspense
_____ leave an impact
_____ lead into the content
_____ rhetorical question
_____ motivate audience to act
_____ startling statement

Get with a classmate and compare your answers.

Do you always agree? If not, why not?

Are there one or two items that are likely to be used in both introductions and in conclusions? Why?

Activity 10: Evaluate an Introduction. Another way to help you be prepared for EFT#4 is to read the following story and evaluate it as an introduction.

Herbert Richey in a speech titled "The Real Causes of Inflation" began with the following. (For the full speech see Richey, H. (1976-77). The real causes of inflation. Vital Speeches of the Day, 43, 386.)

Jed is a part-time farm worker with a flair for applied economics. One day he "borrowed" a country ham from the farmer who employs him…without bothering to tell the farmer.

He went downtown and sold the ham for the grocer for $27. Then he used $20 of that money to buy $80 worth of food stamps.

With the food stamps he bought $48 worth of groceries. He used the remaining $32 worth of food stamps to buy back the ham.

He then returned the ham to the farmer's smokehouse.

So the grocer made a profit, the farmer got his ham back, and Jed has $48 worth of groceries plus $7 in cash.

If you see no flaw in that process, then you are already familiar with modern economics.

On the other hand, if you suspect that someone, somewhere, has been "taken" for $80, then the rest of this speech is dedicated to you.

From *Vital Speeches of the Day*, 43 (1976-1977) 386 by Herbert Richey. Reprinted by permission of City News Publishing Company.

How well did Mr. Richey:

    --Get your attention?

    --Set the tone for the speech?

    --Secure goodwill and respect?

    --Prepare the audience for his main points?

Activity 11: Produce an Introduction. Just to be sure you are ready for the field trip, go back to the outline about Nursing that you unscrambled. You have the outline of the body of the speech. Now produce an introduction for that speech with the city council as your audience.

Activity 12: Produce a Conclusion. Finally, given the review of the goals for a conclusion, produce a conclusion for the speech on Nursing for an audience of state legislators.

Do you feel ready for the field trip? Your pre-trip preparations have included eleven activities. You planned a "dream" trip from San Diego to Bangor, identified the most relevant outcome for EFT#4 in your public speaking syllabus, and examined your knowledge of key concepts by playing the association game. You also reflected upon several patterns for speeches, unscrambled one speech outline, produced a "Spidergram," critiqued an introduction story, and produced both an introduction and a conclusion for the nursing outline

But wait! Is there anything else you would want to do before you leave on the field trip? If so, do it. If you think it might benefit others, jot it down and share it with your instructor and/or classmates. Don't leave home unless your bags are fully packed.

Second Milers: For those who like to go the second mile, excellent additional information about how to create a compelling presentation can be found in the following public speaking textbooks. See chapters 8, 9 & 10 in Brilhart, J. K., Bourhis, J. S., Miley B. R., & Berquist, C. A. (1992). Practical public speaking. New York: HarperCollins; or study chapter 8 in Dance, F. E. X. & Zak-Dance, C. C. (1996). Speaking your mind: Private thinking and public speaking. Dubuque, IA:Kendall/Hunt.

DURING

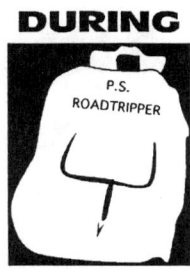

Now that you have made the necessary preparations, let's take the field trip. In this EFT we will visit with an office manager, a supervisor in a library, a news receptionist, an optician, and a retail credit manager. We will ask: **"What do you do to organize your presentations?"**

Take all the notes you desire. Brief notes will enable you to better contribute to discussions with your classmates.

Note which of the following each person addressed. Place a large X under the category for EACH person who mentions that aspect of creating a presentation.

	Arrange-ment	Subor-dination	Coord-ination	Patterns	Purpose	Outline	Body
Office Mgr.							
Library Sprvisor							
News Recept.							
Optician							
Credit Mgr.							

Key points made by each person interviewed.

Office manager:

Library supervisor:

News receptionist:

Optician:

Credit manager:

AFTER
P.S. ROADTRIPPER

Preparation must be made **before** taking a trip and important questions must be asked **during** the trip. But nothing is more important than what happens **after** the trip is over. Critical reflection upon the knowledge gained is what makes all the effort worthwhile.

Reflections. What did you learn from this Electronic Field Trip?

To what extent do these practitioners confirm or illustrate what you read before you took the field trip?

Identify which person in the field trip you believe most insightfully addressed each of the following. Provide reasons for your choices.

Balance–

Arrangement—

Signposting—

Conclusion—

Central idea—

Organizational patterns—

Coordination—

Introduction—

Outlining---

Orderly—

Body--

Transitions---

Who during the EFT best demonstrated they understood the concepts highlighted in EFT# 3--purpose statements (pp. 32-34)? Explain your selection(s).

Get with 3-5 classmates and answer the following questions about EFT#4 itself.

1. What organizational pattern did it follow?

2. How does EFT#4 attempt to gain your attention?

3. Suggest a better way for EFT#4 to meet all the goals of an introduction.

4. Suggest a different arrangement of this field trip. Be specific and provide details.

5. Produce a specific purpose statement for this EFT.

6. Name the course outcome(s) EFT#4 best illustrates and tell why.

Based upon your experiences before, during and after Electronic Field Trip #4, do you feel better equipped to organize a presentation? If so, in what way? If not, why not?

Hometown Newspaper Article. You have been invited by your hometown newspaper to write an advice column for those planning to go to college. Combining your experience on the EFT with all your knowledge about how to organize a presentation, write a brief article that addresses at least three of the following concepts: arrangement patterns, coordination, subordination, functions and types of introductions, functions and types of conclusions, transitions, being orderly, or signposting. Feel free to use the practitioners from the EFT as "eye witness" resources. Your objective is to give aspiring college students tips on studying by showing them that textbooks are organized much like a successful speech. (Your instructor may want to collect these and share a few with the entire class.)

EFT Post Assessment. Finally, what, if anything, would you change about this EFT to make it a better educational experience? Remember that no one can make a better post-assessment of the content and process of this field trip than you, since you took the field trip.

You can now unpack your bags and await your next Electronic Field Trip.

Electronic Field Trip #5
The Importance of Language

You are about to experience an Electronic Field Trip (EFT) with the PS Roadtripper. This field trip is designed to strengthen your ability to utilize language effectively as you prepare presentations. Listen to what former field trip participants have said about EFT#5.

"I learned that in order for people to understanding my perceptions I must pay extra attention to my language."

"I learned that avoiding jargon but repeating the same idea in different words is a good way to increase the understanding of my audience."

"Since listening and speaking are important to advancement in my career field, I learned that I need to pay more attention to my word selection when I give reports or presentations."

"I learned that I have a responsibility as a speaker to be clear and concise so that listeners won't have to wade through lots of clutter."

On EFT#5 you will travel to five interesting and quite unique locations. Like any trip, there are things that must be done **before** leaving, **during** the trip and **after** one returns home. To get ready for EFT#5 you need to complete the following activities and read chapter 13 in Jaffe, C. (1998). <u>Public speaking: Concepts and skills for a diverse society</u> (2nd ed.). Belmont, CA: Wadsworth which addresses the wording of a speech. **Before leaving fill your virtual backpack with the following:**

Activity 1: The Association Game. Play the Association Game. Read the following words or phrases and immediately, without reflection or deliberation, write your initial reactions.

Example: <u>Phrase</u>--Quantum physics   <u>Association</u>--Schroeder's cat

Interesting language–

Cat—

Imagery—

Family—

Euthanasia—

Familiar language—

Cool—

Open—

Vivid language—

The Bomb—

Concrete wording—

Just—

Bubbler—

Clarity of expression—

Bar pit—

Conciseness—

Epistemic—

Appropriate word choices—

Liberal—

Accurate language---

Voice—

Style—

Quack—

Word selection---

Activity 2: Reactions to the Association Experience. In dyads or in small groups, share your reactions to the association experience.

What differences did you notice in the words in the list?

Could you group these words into subsets? If so, how? If not, why not?

Were there any common responses?

Were there some words that meant nothing to you? If so, which?

What did you learn about each other?

What did you learn about the concepts?

What did you learn about the "power" of words to stimulate reactions?

Which words triggered an emotional reaction in you? Why?

Activity 3: M-A-N. Have you ever played with a word by saying it over and over until it literally sounded silly? Well, whether you have or have not, try it. Close your eyes and repeat the word "man" in your head at least 50 times. Do NOT say anything else, just "man." Spell it out—M-A-N. Say it loudly and then softly over and over. Sometimes distort the normal pronunciation—vary the emphasis and pitch. Just keep saying "man" over and over.

How long did it take until it began to sound ridiculous?

What were you thinking while you were doing this?

What were you feeling while you were doing this?

Do you think it would make any difference if you said "anthropos?" How about "hombre?" What about "ahdam?"

All these words have the same referent—a "man." One is Greek, one is Spanish and one is Hebrew. So, what is the point?

--Do you better understand that words are arbitrary? Explain.

--Do you see that words only represent things? Explain.

--Do you understand how the meaning assigned to any utterance depends on the listener not the words themselves? Explain.

--What else did you learn from this exercise?

Activity 4: Levels of Abstraction. Now that you have reacted to and reflected upon your use of words, the next step in the "before" process will focus on the use of words to express different levels of abstraction. Be as deliberate and reflective as possible. Arrange the following lists of words along a continuum from general or abstract to specific or concrete.

Number the items from 1 = most general to 5 = most specific.

GENERAL/ABSTRACT

Dog

An

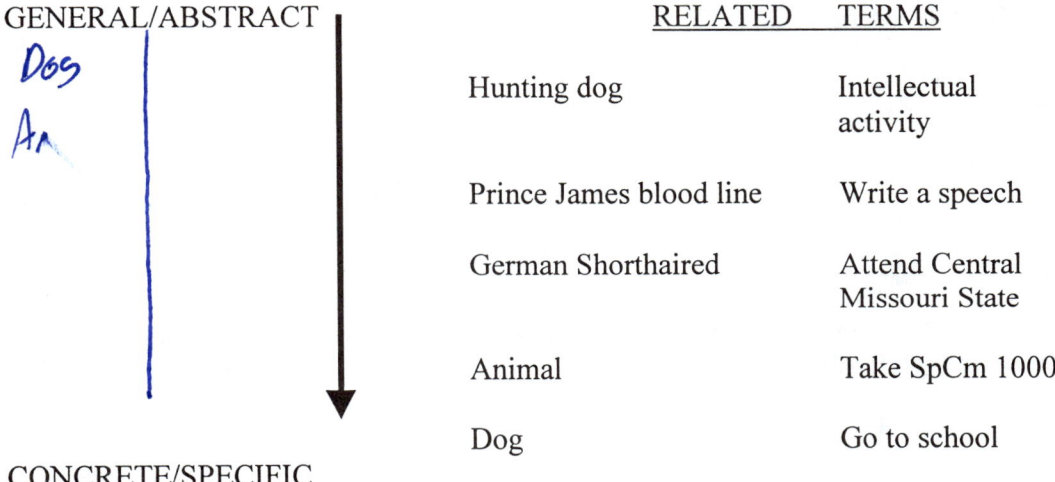

RELATED	TERMS
Hunting dog	Intellectual activity
Prince James blood line	Write a speech
German Shorthaired	Attend Central Missouri State
Animal	Take SpCm 1000
Dog	Go to school

CONCRETE/SPECIFIC

What does the abstract-to-concrete continuum for words have in common with outlining?

Should you use abstract words in a speech? If so, how? If not, why not?

Activity 5: Meaning--Denotative versus Connotative. Another item to check off before leaving on the field trip is a review of denotative and connotative meaning.

Go back to your word association list. What was your **first** reaction to:

Cat?

Euthanasia?

Quack?

Liberal?

Is what you wrote down the denotative or connotative meaning for each word? Explain.

Using the four words of cat, euthanasia, quack and liberal, explain the difference between denotative and connotative meaning.

Has the meaning of any of these four words changed for you? If so, how? If not, provide two examples of words whose meaning has changed for you.

Activity 6: Style--Written versus Oral. Have you ever heard anyone read a speech and noted that it sounded like an essay rather than a speech? Why do you think that happened?

Compare the following examples from Gronbeck, B., Ehninger, D., Monroe, A. H., & German, K. (1988). Principles of speech communication (10th ed.). Glenview, IL: Scott, Foresman, p. 177.

--Written Style--

I am most pleased that you could come this morning. I would like to use this opportunity to discuss with you a subject of inestimable importance to us all—the impact of inflationary spirals on students enrolled in institutions of higher education.

--Oral Style--

Thanks for coming. I'd like to talk today about something that everyone here has had experience with—the rising costs of going to college.

What are some key differences in the two styles of presentation?

Even though the oral style is less formal, clarity of expression is always important. The paragraph below contains a great deal of clutter, unnecessary words and phrases, that even confuse the issue. Read through the following paragraph and eliminate the clutter. Make the paragraph more concise and easily understood.

There is nothing in the ~~whole wide~~ ok world that is more ~~wonderfully~~ appetizing than a fresh baked ~~brand new~~ warm loaf of ~~home-made~~ bread. And when you happen to own a breadmaker it is ~~simply~~ easy to make fresh bread. And what's ~~even~~ better is the machine does ~~most of~~ the the work automatically. To begin to start baking you will need a ~~simple~~ receipe. First, mix the ~~non-dry~~ liquid ingredients in the baking tube. These might be warm water, lemon juice, oil or applesauce if you are "cutting the fat" and ~~prefer to eat fat-free bread~~. Then, in a separate bowl ~~other than the baking tube~~, mix the dry ingredients like flour, salt, sugar and dry not whole milk. Pour these on top of the liquid ingredients. Dig out a small hole in the center and add the yeast. ~~down in th~~ere. Place the baking tube in the machine. Pick out the settings you desire and push ~~on~~ the buttons. In three or four hours, the baked bread is done and ready to eat, ~~and enjoy~~. Adding butter and jam will make it an extra special treat!

Compare your rewrite with at least one other person's and see who best clarified the message by eliminating needless verbiage without distorting the message.

Activity 7: Producing Similes. The final step in your preparation is to practice creating vivid expressions. Do you remember Forrest Gump's statement that "Life is like a box of chocolates?" That helped the viewers have a vivid image of what he was trying to express. You can do the same thing. Brainstorm 5 or 6 endings to the following statement.

"This class is like…"

Next, select **one** of your similes and extend it by generating 3 or 4 reasons why. For example, "This class is like a lemon pie **because** sometimes it is sweet, sometimes it is sour, but it is always filling."

This class is like _____ **because**…

Are you ready for the field trip? Your before preparations have included seven valuable activities. You explored how words are arbitrary and representative, experienced different levels of familiarity with words, and explored trigger words via the association game. You also ranked words from most abstract to least abstract. In addition, you discussed the difference between denotative and connotative meaning, compared oral and written language styles, and worked as an editor to insure clarity and conciseness. Finally, you produced one simile with its attendant because statements.

But wait! Is there anything else you would want to do before you leave on the field trip? If so, do it. If you think it might benefit others, jot it down and share it with your instructor and/or classmates. Don't leave home unless your bags are fully packed.

Second Milers: For those who like to go the second mile, excellent additional information about how to use language to produce a captivating presentation can be found in the following public speaking textbooks. See chapter 11 in Lucas, S. E. (1995). <u>The art of public speaking</u> (5th ed.). New York: McGraw Hill; or study chapter 8 in Gronbeck, B., Ehninger, D., Monroe, A. H., & German, K. (1988). Principles of speech communication (10th ed.). Glenview, IL: Scott, Foresman.

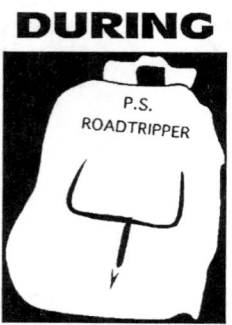

Now that you have made the necessary preparations, let's take the field trip.
In this EFT we will visit with a graphic designer and animator, a production assistant, a videographer and production specialist, an independent sales representative, and an education coordinator for a salon supply company. We will ask: **"How do you use language to insure you give an effective presentation?"**

Take all the notes you desire. Brief notes will enable you to better contribute to discussions with your classmates.

Note which of the following each person addressed. Place a large X under the category for EACH person who mentions that aspect of creating a presentation.

	Vivid	Concrete	Clear	Concise	Approp.	Accurate
Animator						
Product. Assistant						
Video-Grapher						
Sales Rep.						
Education Coord.						

Key points made by each person interviewed.

Graphic designer/animator:

Production assistant:

Videographer/production specialist:

Independent sales representative:

AFTER

Preparation must be made **before** taking the trip and important questions must be asked **during** the field trip. But nothing is more important than what happens **after** the field trip. Critical reflection upon the knowledge gained is what makes all the effort worthwhile.

Reflections. What did you learn from this Electronic Field Trip?

To what extent do these practitioners confirm or illustrate what you read before you took the field trip?

Identify which person in the field trip you believe most insightfully addressed each of the following. Provide reasons for your choices.

Interesting language–

Interesting language–

Imagery—

Familiar language—

Vivid language—

Concrete wording—

Clarity of expression—

Conciseness—

Appropriate word choices—

Accurate language---

Style—

Word selection---

Who during EFT#5 best demonstrated they understood the role of language in writing a captivating presentation? Explain your selection(s).

Based upon your experiences before, during and after Electronic Field Trip #5, are you better prepared to effectively word a speech? If so, in what way? If not, why not?

Hometown Newspaper Article. You have been invited by your hometown newspaper to write an advice column for those planning to go to college. Combine your experiences on EFT#5 with all your knowledge about the roles and functions of language in a speech. Write a brief article that addresses at least three of the following language concepts: imagery, familiarity, interesting, vivid, concrete, clear, concise, appropriate, accurate, and style. Feel free to use the practitioners from the EFT as "eye witness" resources. Your objective is to convince your readers that attention to language is important and that developing a wide vocabulary is essential to success in college. (Your instructor may want to collect these and share a few with the entire class.)

EFT Post Assessment. Finally, what, if anything, would you change about this EFT to make it a better educational experience? Remember that no one can make a better post-assessment of the content and process of this field trip than you, since you took the field trip.

You can now unpack your bags and await your next Electronic Field Trip.

Electronic Field Trip #6
Delivering a Speech

You are about to experience an Electronic Field Trip (EFT) with the PS Roadtripper. This field trip is designed to help equip you to deliver a speech. Listen to what former field trip participants have said about EFT#6.

"Speaking so people understand you and making eye contact increases credibility. Being very knowledgeable about what you are speaking also helps."

"I learned that the way you present your information (vocal and eye contact) is as important as the information itself."

"You need to be prepared since the tone, vocabulary and eye contact are very important. Be honest and trustworthy since your word is your bond."

"You need to adjust your voice to fit whoever you are speaking and to stress whatever you want to stress. Your voice can indicate how the rest of your interaction will go. Don't use jargon."

On EFT#6 you will travel to six interesting and quite unique locations. Like any trip, there are things that must be done **before** leaving, **during** the trip and **after** one returns home. To get ready for EFT#6 you need to complete the following activities and read chapter 14 in Jaffe, C. (1998). <u>Public speaking: Concepts and skills for a diverse society</u> (2nd ed.). Belmont, CA: Wadsworth, which addresses the delivery of a speech. **Before leaving fill your virtual backpack with the following:**

Activity 1: The Association Game. Read the following words or phrases and immediately, without reflection or deliberation, write your initial reactions.

Example: Word--poise   Association--speaking with confidence

Eye contact–

Audiovisuals/technology—

Gestures—

Relaxation techniques—

Visualization—

Voice—

Articulation—

Be yourself—

Memoria—

Rehearse—

Elocution—

Activity 2: Reactions to the Association Experience. In dyads or in small groups, share your reactions to the association experience.

What differences did you notice in the way each reacted to the words in the list?

Were there any common responses?

Were there some words that meant nothing to you? If so, which?

What did you learn about each other?

What did you learn about the concepts?

What ideas or questions about delivering a speech did this stimulate?

Activity 3: Types of Delivery. Now that you have reacted to and reflected upon some key concepts related to speech delivery, the next step will focus on types of delivery.*

Match the following types of delivery with their descriptions.

_____ reading from a manuscript   1. Impromptu

_____ memorization of the speech word for word   2. Extemporaneous

_____ without prior rehearsal   3. Manuscript

_____ speaking from an outline   4. Memorized

Identify which type of delivery would be most appropriate for each of the following situations.

_____ speaking before a congressional hearing   1. Impromptu

_____ speaking to a high school senior class about college   2. Extemporaneous

_____ speaking to a group of fraternity or sorority members 3. Manuscript

_____ speaking to the combined state legislature   4. Memorized

_____ a student responding to a question by a professor

_____ speaking at synagogue, mosque or church

_____ speaking in class

_____ speaking during a question and answer session

Be prepared to explain WHY you matched each situation above as you did.

*To check the correctness of your answers see chapter 14 in Jaffe, C. (1998). <u>Public speaking: Concepts and skills for a diverse society</u> (2nd ed.). Belmont, CA: Wadsworth.

Activity 4: Do's and Don'ts. Now that you have reflected upon the types of delivery, evaluate the following lists of "Do's" and "Don'ts" during the actual delivery.

Write DO or DON'T in front of each of the following.

_____ display poise

_____ write on the back of note cards

_____ drum your fingers on the lectern

_____ establish good eye contact

_____ let your hair cover your eyes

_____ become familiar with the content of your speech

_____ stand straight

_____ rehearse every detail of the physical delivery of your speech

_____ lift your notes from the lectern

_____ chew gum

_____ sway or bounce on the hip

_____ position shoulders parallel to the floor

_____ flip your head to rearrange your hair

_____ show adverse, nonpurposeful facial expressions

_____ establish good eye contact

_____ keep both feet on the floor

_____ use unrelated hand movements

_____ lay your hands on the back of the lectern

_____ grasp the sides of the lectern

_____ use a variety of gestures

_____ cross your legs behind the lectern

_____ keep your notes flat on the lectern

_____ slide your notes aside as you progress

_____ vary the position of your hands throughout

_____ approach the lectern while mumbling and expressing uncertainty

_____ pause and take a deep breath before your first word

_____ pause for one full count before leaving the lectern

_____ distribute your eye contact throughout the room

_____ panic if you forget something

_____ use pauses to regain your composure

_____ always begin by apologizing

_____ pace back and forth in front of the audience

_____ shift your weight from one leg to the other instead of pacing

Activity 5: Vocal Behavior. Vocal behavior is another vital element in the delivery of a presentation. Complete the following to refresh your memory and enhance your readiness for EFT#6.

Read the following sentences out loud and stress the capitalized and underlined word each time.

    <u>HE"S</u> giving this money to Katie.

He's <u>GIVING</u> this money to Katie.

He's giving <u>THIS</u> money to Katie.

He's giving this <u>MONEY</u> to Katie.

He's giving this money <u>TO</u> Katie.

He's giving this money to <u>KATIE</u>.

What did you learn from this? What are possible applications of this exercise to your next speech?

Have you ever heard an audio or video recording of a presentation you have given? Did it sound "different?" You were hearing yourself via air conduction, the way other people hear you. Normally, we hear ourselves by means of bone conduction. But the uniqueness of your vocal qualities is a blessing not a hindrance. Read the article by Yan Hong Krompacky.

"Immigrants Don't Be in Such a Hurry to Shed Your Accents"

To the Editor:

You report that immigrants in New York City are turning to speech classes to reduce the sting of discrimination against them based on accent....I'd like to tell all my fellow immigrants taking accent-reduction classes: As long as you speak fluent and comprehensible English, don't waste your money on artificially removing your accent.

I am fortunate enough to be one of the linguistically gifted. I even acquired an American accent before I left China for the United States five years ago. From the day I set foot on this continent till now, the praise of my English has never ceased. What most people single out is that I have no or very little accent. However, I know I *do* have an accent.... I intend to keep it because it belongs to me. I want to speak and write grammatically flawless English, but I have no desire to equip myself with a perfect American accent....

America is probably the largest place for accents in English because the entire nation is composed of immigrants from different areas of the world. This country is built on accents. Accent is one of the most conspicuous symbols of what makes America the free and prosperous land its own people are proud of and other people long to live in.

I work in an urban institution where accents are an integral part of my job: students, faculty and staff come from ethnically diverse backgrounds. Hearing accents confirms for me every day that the college is fulfilling its goal to offer education to a multicultural population.

I wonder what accent my fellow immigrants should obtain after getting rid of their own: a New York accent? A Boston accent? Brooklyn? Texas? California? Or go after President Clinton's accent?

Fellow immigrants, don't worry about the way you speak until Peter Jennings eliminates his Canadian accent.

>   Yan Hong Krompacky
>   Letter to the Editor
>   The New York Times, March 21, 1993
>   Adapted by Clella Jaffe.

From *The New York Times*, Editorial Page, March 21, 1993.

Do you agree or disagree with Yan Hong? Explain why.

According to Yan Hong what attention should be given to enunciation and pronunciation?

Activity 6: Anxiety. Your virtual backpack is almost loaded. There is only one item left—how you feel about giving a speech. Almost everyone feels some anxiety prior to and during oral presentations. Some people are bothered much more than others. Therefore, before you leave on the field trip, some reflection is in order.

First, if you feel much anxiety, what do you do to help manage it?

Have you ever tried taking a couple very very slow and deep breaths just before you get up to give the speech? What about after you set down your notes and position yourself in front of your audience? Watch for any comments by the practitioners about relaxation strategies.

Finally, remember the difference thorough preparation will make. Write the speech a week or so before you present it. Practice giving your speech out loud to different people. Practice in the exact place you will give the speech if possible. If not, find a place as similar as is possible. Again, watch for what the people interviewed have to say about practice.

Are you ready for the field trip? Your before preparations have included seven helpful actions. You thought about some key concepts, examined different types of delivery and assessed when each is most appropriate. You distinguished between a bunch of "do's" and "don'ts' of delivery and experienced the impact of vocal stress on suggested meaning. Next, you reflected upon the relationship between an individual accent and the need for clear pronunciation and enunciation. Finally, you considered strategies to manage harmful levels of speech anxiety

But wait! Is there anything else you would want to do before you leave on the field trip? If so, do it. If you think it might benefit others, jot it down and share it with your instructor and/or classmates. Don't leave home unless your virtual bags are fully packed.

Second Milers: For those who like to go the second mile, excellent additional information about how to effectively deliver a presentation can be found in the following public speaking textbooks. See chapters 14-17 in Kearney, P., & Plax, T. G. (1996). Public speaking in a diverse society. Mountain View, CA: Mayfield; or study chapter 12 in Zarefsky, D. (1996). Public speaking: Strategies for success. Boston: Allyn & Bacon.

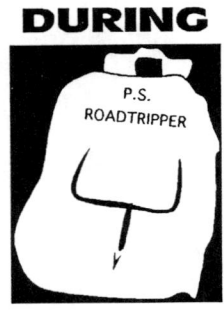

DURING

Now that you have made the necessary preparations, let's take the field trip. On this EFT we will visit with an independent financial consultant, a retail credit manager, a news receptionist, an optician, a production technician/engineer, and the owner of an international sports marketing firm. We will ask: **"What advice would you give someone regarding the actual delivery of a speech?"**

Take all the notes you desire. Brief notes will enable you to better contribute to discussions with your classmates.

Note which of the following each person addresses. Place a large X under the category for EACH person who mentions that aspect of delivery.

	Practice	Relax	Voice	Gestures	Visuals
Consultant					
Manager					
Reception.					
Optician					
Engineer					
Owner					

Key points made by each person interviewed.

Independent financial consultant:

Retail credit manager:

News receptionist & assistant:

Optician:

Production Technician/Engineer:

Owner of sports marketing firm:

Preparation must be made **before** taking the trip and important questions must be asked **during** the field trip. But nothing is more important than what happens **after** the trip is over. Critical reflection upon the knowledge gained is what makes all the effort worthwhile.

Reflections. What did you learn from this Electronic Field Trip?

To what extent do these practitioners confirm or illustrate what you read before you took the field trip?

Identify which person in the field trip you believe most insightfully addressed each of the following. Provide reasons for your choices.

Eye contact–

Audiovisuals/technology—

Gestures—

Relaxation techniques—

Visualization—

Voice—

Articulation—

Be yourself—

Memoria—

Rehearse—

Elocution—

Who during EFT#6 provided you with the most helpful advice regarding the delivery of a speech? Explain your selection(s).

What questions would you like to ask these practitioners now that you are home from the field trip?

Based upon your experiences before, during and after Electronic Field Trip #6, do you believe you are better prepared to deliver your next speech? If so, in what way? If not, why not?

Hometown Newspaper Article. You have been invited by your hometown newspaper to write an advice column for those planning to go to college. Combine your experiences on EFT#6 with all your knowledge of and experience with actually delivering a speech. Write a brief article that addresses at least three of the following delivery concepts: articulation, be yourself, visualize, gestures, eye contact, voice, audiovisuals/technology, rehearsal, relaxation techniques and note cards. Feel free to use the practitioners from the EFT as "eye witness" resources. Use your knowledge of delivering a speech to advise new college students on how to make new friends and give good "first" impressions. (Your instructor may want to collect these and share a few with the entire class.)

EFT Post Assessment. Finally, what, if anything, would you change about this EFT to make it a better educational experience? Remember that no one can make a better post-assessment of the content and process of this field trip than you, since **you** took the field trip.

You can now unpack your virtual backpack and await your next Electronic Field Trip.

Electronic Field Trip #7
Analyzing Your Audience

You are about to experience an Electronic Field Trip (EFT) with the PS Roadtripper. This field trip is designed to help equip you to deliver a speech. Listen to what former field trip participants have said about EFT#7.

"I learned to think about how my subject will relate to my audience."

"I learned that it is important to figure out what they want so you will know what kind of thing to offer. It is also important to get the input of others before telling them what to do."

"I learned the importance of audience involvement in the speech-making process."

"I learned that it is important in many job areas to be able to deliver a persuasive speech."

On EFT#7 you will travel to the work sites of five professionals. Like any field trip, there are things that must be done **before** leaving, **during** the trip and **after** one returns home. To get ready for EFT#7 you need to complete the following activities and read chapter 5 in Jaffe, C. (1998). <u>Public speaking: Concepts and skills for a diverse society</u> (2nd ed.). Belmont, CA: Wadsworth. **Before leaving fill your virtual backpack with the following:**

Activity 1: The Association Game. Read the following words or phrases and immediately, without reflection or deliberation, write your initial reactions.

Example: Phrase--partisan audience   Association--preaching to the choir

Interest–

Knowledge—

Attitudes toward the speaker—

Attitudes toward the topic—

Motivation—

Composition—

Beliefs—

Invention—

Disposition—

Passive—

Ethnicity—

Group affiliations—

Values—

Socio-cultural status—

Demographics—

Activity 2: Reactions to the Association Experience. In dyads or in small groups, share your reactions to the association experience.

What differences did you notice in the way each reacted to the words in the list?

Were there any common responses?

Were there some words that meant nothing to you? If so, which?

What did you learn about each other?

What did you learn about the concepts?

What ideas or questions about analyzing an audience did this stimulate?

Activity 3: Audience Adaptation. Now that you have reacted to and reflected upon some key concepts related to analyzing an audience, the next step in the "before" process will focus on exploring the key elements in audience adaptation.

Compare and contrast these two definitions of audience adaptation.

> "Its ultimate goal is to determine what kind of message (if any) will be most likely to achieve a given purpose with a particular audience: but, first looks at the characteristics of the listeners and the speaking situation." (Ellingsworth, H.W. & Clevenger, T. (1967). Speech and social action: A strategy of oral communication. Englewood, NJ: Prentice-Hall, p. 105.)

> "Above all, it means two things: (a) assessing how your audience is likely to respond to what you will say in your speech and (b) adjusting what you say to make it as clear, appropriate, and convincing as possible." (Lucas, S. E. (1995). The art of public speaking. New York: McGraw-Hill, p. 109.)

In what ways are they alike?

In what ways are they different?

Activity 4: Attitudes and Group Affiliations. Our attitudes toward particular ideas can be placed along a continuum that ranges from fanatically in favor to fanatically opposed. Using the following list of statements, **identify groups with which a person would likely be affiliated** if they are either "In Favor Of" or "Opposed To" the statement. Place the group along the continuum where you think they best fit.

⬅—————————————————————————➡

Fanatically In Favor   Fanatically Opposed

Smoking

Handguns

Alcohol

Abortion

Animal Rights

Body Piercing

Activity 5: Features of an Audience Analysis. The next preparation activity is to use the following six features of an audience analysis to identify what is being sought by each of the statements/questions.*

A. Knowledge   D. Beliefs

B. Interest   E. Values

C. Attitudes   F. Demographics

_____ I have friends who are farmers.   _____ The government is too involved in the agricultural industry.

101

_____ I don't feel agriculture has any effect on me.

_____ Do you know what tracking is?

_____ How would you feel if your child was placed into a lower ability class?

_____ Do you think tracking is a fair way to educate children?

_____ I would be interested in knowing more about social welfare.

_____ The majority of welfare recipients are unwed mothers.

_____ Welfare, or public assistance, is a "right" that should be afforded to anyone who is in need.

_____ Marijuana should be legalized.

_____ Products with hemp leaf on them should be banned from schools.

_____ I consider myself informed on the various sides of the issue of carrying concealed weapons.

_____ Circle male or female.

_____ Do you believe healthcare reform is important?

_____ Should healthcare reform be a national priority?

_____ Are you a fan of college sports?

_____ When is a fetus considered to be a human life?

_____ Would you like information on being a vegetarian?

_____ Could you give up just red meat?

_____ What would the reaction be in your house if you couldn't have meat for a week?

_____ Should be get "tough" on juvenile crime?

_____ Does Missouri have a law to automatically certify juveniles as adults when a serious crime is committed?

_____ Is justice served best when a juvenile is tried as an adult when they commit a serious crime?

_____ In your opinion, do you feel rehabilitation is more effective than incarceration for serious juvenile offenders?

_____ Do you believe that deer hunting is cruel and should be outlawed?

_____ An unemployed mother of six is waiting at home patiently to receive a check from your tax money. Is this fair?

*To check your answers see the readings for Second Milers.

Activity 6: Persuasive Speech Evaluation Form. Finally, evaluate the following Persuasive Speech Evaluation Form from Cox, E.S. & Adams, W. C. (1990, August). A proposal to better define persuasive speaking: Audience parameters. Paper presented at the Second Individual Events Conference, Denver, CO.

<u>Persuasive Speech Evaluation Form</u> --Rank the speaker, 10=superbly and 1 = not at all

Did the speaker make appropriate adjustments for image?

Did the arrangement reflect a sensitivity to the audience's attitudinal predisposition?

Was the speaker's goal realistic given the audience's characteristics?

Were reservations meaningfully presented and dealt with for this audience?

Did the speech reflect an awareness of the audience's pre-existing knowledge?

Were appeals directed to the audience's motives?

Were social constraints apparently considered in the development of this speech?

Is the form adequate? Explain.

Does it assess adaptations before as well as during the speech? Explain.

What, if anything, should be changed? Suggest improvements.

Are you ready for the field trip? Your **before** preparations have included six activities. You thought about some key concepts, compared two definitions of audience adaptation, and identified groups and rated their likely stance on controversial issues. You matched questions or statements with five features of an audience analysis and evaluated audience adaptation features of a persuasive speech form.

But wait! Is there anything else you would want to do before you leave on the field trip? If so, do it. If you think it might benefit others, jot it down and share it with your instructor and/or classmates. Don't leave home unless your virtual bags are fully packed.

Second Milers: For those who like to go the second mile, excellent additional information about how to effectively analyze an audience can be found in the following public speaking textbooks. See chapter 4 in Osborn, M. & Osborn, S. (1994). Public speaking (3rd ed.). Boston: Houghton Mifflin; study chapter 4 in Lucas, S. E. (1995). The art of public speaking. New York: McGraw-Hill; or read chapters 5 & 6 in Ellingsworth, H. W. & Clevenger, T. (1967). Speech and social action: A strategy of oral communication. Englewood Cliffs, NJ: Prentice-Hall.

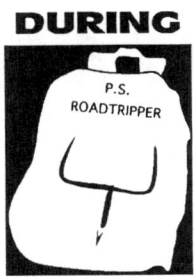

DURING

P.S. ROADTRIPPER

Now that you have made the necessary preparations, let's take the field trip. On this EFT we will visit with a district manager, a director of technical staffing, a production technician/engineer, the owner of an international sports marketing firm, and a homemaker and swim coach. We will ask: **"When preparing for a presentation, what is important to know about your audience?"**

Take all the notes you desire. Brief notes will enable you to better contribute to discussions with your classmates.

Note which of the following each person addresses. Place a large X under the category for EACH person who mentions that aspect of delivery.

	Interest	Knowledge	Attitudes	Affiliations	Demo-graphics
Manager					
Director					
Engineer					
Owner					
Homemaker					

Key points made by each person interviewed.

District Manager:

Director of Technical Staffing:

Technician/Engineer

Owner of International Sports Marketing firm:

Homemaker and swim coach:

> Preparation must be made **before** taking the trip and important questions must be asked **during** the field trip. But nothing is more important than what happens **after** the field trip. Critical reflection upon the knowledge gained is what makes all the effort worthwhile.

Reflections. What did you learn from this Electronic Field Trip?

To what extent do these practitioners confirm or illustrate what you read before you took the field trip?

Identify which person in the field trip you believe most insightfully addressed each of the following. Provide reasons for your choices.

Interest–

Knowledge—

Attitudes toward the speaker—

Attitudes toward the topic—

Motivation—

Composition—

Beliefs—

Invention—

Disposition—

Passive—

Ethnicity—

Group affiliations—

Values—

Socio-cultural status—

Demographics—

Who during EFT#7 provided you with the most helpful advice regarding adapting messages to fit your audience? Explain your selection(s).

What questions would you like to ask these practitioners now that you are home from the field trip?

Tailoring a Topic for Different Audiences. How would you tailor a speech on the topic of food for the following audiences?

- High school sophomores in a mandatory assembly

- Senior citizens during a voluntary special program

- Student dietitians at a regional workshop

- College football players at a meeting called by the weight coach

Based upon your experiences before, during and after Electronic Field Trip #7, what will you do to prepare for your next speech? Explain why.

Hometown Newspaper Article. You have been invited by your hometown newspaper to write an advice column for those planning to go to college. Utilize your experiences related to EFT#7 and write a brief article that addresses at least three of the following adaptation concepts: Interest, knowledge, attitudes toward the speaker, attitudes toward the topic, motivation, composition, beliefs, passive audience, ethnicity, group affiliations, values, socio-cultural status, or demographics. Feel free to use the practitioners from the EFT as "eye witness" resources. Your objective is to discuss several groups or "audiences" that new college students may encounter. Advise them how to adapt. (Your instructor may want to collect these and share a few with the entire class.)

EFT Post Assessment. Finally, what, if anything, would you change about this EFT to make it a better educational experience? Remember that no one can make a better post-assessment of the content and process of this field trip than you, since you took the field trip.

You can now unload your backpack and await your next Electronic Field Trip.